fullstop Fascism

m.c. k⁹

12/8 Path Publications

ISBN 978-0-578-22171-7

Contents

focus on Fascism

why do it in poetic form?
because in an infinite variety of ways
that reside in the breasts of all living souls
any solution to the Fascist trend in all states
pulses and grooves inside each of us
we hear the basic call to consciousness & conscience

to free our selves from fundi-Xtian fascists,
we have to free them from their selfish selves
to free our selves from islamofascists technofascists progressofascists
we have to free our selves first
to "go global & go local"
to "chill globally and groove locally"
to *be* effective & reveal our essence in every song and dance routine
          and *HAVE* nothing
asserting & affirming in every celebration of the moment
          every party every feast every fierce enjoyment of the moment

focus on Fascism

unstoppable Fascism rolls along as if it were reality and not a bad dream
the emerging left-right alliance is not emerging fast enough
     an alliance sounds temporary a matter of convenience a united affront
to dissmantle the corporate state
          means to take the mantle or cloak off   remove its cover
               "de-face the currency"
          find the means to take civ apart piece by piece
                    one small "convergence" of libs and cons after another

this might work if we can just focus on the F word for a few moments
          at different times
of each day whaddayasay? Fasc a bundle of twigs wrapped around an ax
     how strong is the string?
     is it a leather thong that shrinks   dries out   might snap?
the twigs are tightly tangled remove the string   the bundle holds or folds
                         one snip of the dialectical scissors!
                    might big twigs turn to sawdust in our hands?

Modern No. 20

eden ahbez, who gave us "Nature Boy" for nat king cole to sing, believed
that only God and Infinity deserve capitalization
m.c. k⁹ plays and prays for Gaia & Eternity as near equivalence in 2019

Fascism and especially Techno-Fascism [in Modern No. 20 the numbers
and the CAPITALIST Capitals are so heavy] we imprison the news in
brackets
[Der Fuhrer is Linear Minded.
                is One Flesh One Bone One Blood One Cuntry #1 One Flag.
                is Goald Directed.
                is One together with those not afraid to die
                            for Deutschland. Fodderland. Patrisnarky.
                                        Uber Alles]

now   in present time
& forever in Gaia & Eternity
        we affirm life in all its processes

Homo Sap Sap: knowing explains our very BEING it's all we are or ever will be
the worst is behind us and we will get even better than this
action is the attraction   hand in the air like you just don't care — Sig Heil
we sit around the great inclusive round table where there is no class
or caste
                                        in the   Equality of Death

punctuation

The end-product of an artist's work,
the "useful commodity" in the production of which he plays a role,
is ideological influence.

He is as incapable of producing this on his own as a blacksmith is of producing Concorde.
The production of ideological influence is highly socialized
involving (in the case of music) performers, critics, impresarios, agents, managers, etc.,
and above all
(and this is the artist's real "means of production")
an audience.
> —Cornelius Cardew, *Stockhausen Serves Imperialism*, June 14, 1974

Above the commas are related to question marks
                                the parentheses are sun and moon
cradling the real

                & the fullstop is fullstop "i conquer"

                            •

american type writer

for this morning's F word medication-meditation
some junkture phenomena
                              this american type writer
feels the pull the tug to just shut up and lay low
boy do i like the feel of one syll-a-ble at a time
on the page full stop on a dime
lord free me from sleaze free me from the slime
call me to breakfast one bite at a time

why I dislike Conspiracy Theorists

They take agency away from both victims and executioners.

They think the reality they imagine is both bigger
and worse than my reality,
when in fact the Horosho of American Fascism/Imperialism/Racism
killing Nature's Gaia "by accident" is much worse
than anything they can imagine being conspired by dark forces

the only difference between our technofascism and Hitler's is that he
used science and technology to "cleanse" the world of jews, gypsies, slavs,
queers, lefties, disabled (people more creative, imaginative, life-loving
than the Nazi),
whereas we are using science and technology to wipe out Nature Herself

                                        GAIA
                                        GE as in geography

and therefore us
we Her peoples

dear editors of m.c. k⁹

goals of these works:

to prove & improve the groove

to provoke the foke, push many more people to fill up pages
with word play

within this broad movement, to celebrate idiosyncrasy, individuation,
the megalomaniacal, grandiose, founding/inventing of local religions,
mystical cults, many little "schools" of "fishes," clusters of totems,
clumps of taboos, gaggles of gag writers, jiggles of jokesters, groupings of
snoopings

to promote m.c. k⁹'s theory of R.G.T. Above's practice of punctuation as a
personal *deeper power* messaging mode of directed symbolism
(a reader of these pages could be thinking that any colon might be a
gypsy fullstop "dark dictum" or its opposite, a "light equalization" of
whatever follows the :)

to synthesize or blend (rather than analyze, take apart) words into new
meanings e.g. "smugnorant"

to repeat punning formulas in a variety of contexts so they take on layer
after layer of meaning increasing their mojo and power as we go along

does your line of poetry "make the drummer sound good"

post-drumpf, post-brewski-brett, post-pomononsense, post-
Ishothiminselfdefense, post pity party po me po me po me another drink,
post being a post on the way there, post-posting posties on facebook, post
postits on the fridge door, post all the deplorables tweets galore?

permanent state of mine

drumpf dream that knew itself as dream from very near the start
knew itself as impossible to smash by the dreamer no waking possible
endless replication of replicants in room after room after room because
each room open and in process one for women in their fifties aching
to stay 18 forever and ever never leaving never straying never arriving
at 19 or 20 always breeding for the fatherland and all the men above
average 2

it was okay that nothing could wake me or shake me or hurt me as
witness to experiments in prosthetics and extensions like atlatls for
hurling @ churls every kind of innovation unchecked by "public safety"
public peeking in the chambers and endless labs were always in the
process of setting up or taking down fresh achievements fresh
experiments bright & glossy drumpf passing through on the way to
another outrageous engagement

disappearing out a far door as I entered unexpected and ignored not
wanted for this experiment or any of the others either not needed to be
exceeded finally stopped trying to get out of this dream so far in the
future drumpf racing to a conclusion of the transformation into
greatness, firstness, exceptional normality everything ours for the
taking because we wanted replication wanted to make ourselves
permanent in growth permanent in firstness

Vote Your Fears and Watch FER Factors Flourish

All Caps for Big Capitalism Hip Flip Hooray
lower case for bell hooks, k d lang, e e cummings on a good hair day

FER = Fascist Ethnocentric Racism, the deadliest form of discrimination
leads to gulags and guantanamos and endless resentments recrimination

let us deFER gratifications, live simply, don't consume

what we lose in power we gain in elegance

perennial grains

        no plow agric
           less wind and water erosion
              top soil deepening a big gain

   [[brackets] are for hiving off, containing the wrong turn or
misstake on reality]

     {{braces} are bracing, bolstering, what's within immanent & ready to
push outward in both or all directions, the arrow within the bow potentiating
abrasively, overshooting any obstacles}}

((gypsy fullstop's (sun&moon)), nurturing arms, cradling, sustaining,
benign reality, cosmic reassurance) a "mutually responsive interdependence"

something very good is happening that helps me keep the Faith in
humanity co-evolving with the rest of the speciation
we can nurture, along with an improved "perennial philosophy,"
the healing, the reforesting, the permaculture & perennial grains & & &

crystal clear

face it we were never great
it was always about murdering innocents
for the state
the 2nd amendment meant to mask
murder and mayhem
rationalized the multiple genocides
of indigenous tribes
and prepared for the suppression of slave revolts
corpses piling up in stacks

though crystal clear
is the prose syntax
          "A well regulated militia . . . ."
NRA ignores these facts

Death Sentence

Every sentence is a death sentence. [Fullstop Conquers.]

    language shapes culture shapes personality shapes a one-person world

anytime we will let it   anytime you dear reader declare it

meeting

erika & ursula, 89 and 88,
meeting for the first time
from either side of the Holocaust
looked at a photo album
of Nazis at a resort in 1944
partying at Auschwitz

eden

eden
Eternity
equality
essence

a throwback   a last hurra   a recapitulation   a kind of grace that can
not   save this state as "nation"

birds

turn the pigeons loose! & the blue jays
        the ravens striding
woodpeckers: downie
                hairy
                red headed
                        golden breasted up from oklahoma and texas
nuthatches
        mr fllcker

why would steve and greg and gil and wanda all die young? it feels like
these were the students I couldn't teach how to live. they all wanted to
help me to help them. not clear enough about intent. in retrospect it feels
like they were in flight from progress and civilization and couldn't get to
the shelters quick enough. were grabbed from behind.

Number 2

Optimism:
(1. hopeful, cheerful, thinking positive about outcomes, generalized optimism.)

(2. the doctrine, especially as set forth by Leibniz, that this world is the best of all possible worlds.)

The problem is we took a wrong turn:
    into so-called "civilization and progress" just a few millennia ago
    into so-called "industrial civilization and progress" just a few centuries ago
    into technofascism, corruption, decay, commodification of everything, alienation of everyone, just a generation ago
    into over-stretched "carrying capacity," over-shot populations, over-plundered, overconsumed, overwhelmed Nature just a few days, months, or years ago

The only way to get some Optimism #1 back is to think big about going small-is-necessary & small-is-beautiful in local peace economies where a small and "Permanent Autonomous Zone" (PAZ or PEACE) economic base is shaping local song-dance-drummings, local social aid and pleasure club brass banding, local permaculture reforestings, local perennial gardening, enlarging the local commons, preserving local foods in local coolers, steadily enhancing a local energy grid using sun, wind, and water, reopening what has been "enclosed," reviving local forms of spirituality and subsistence horticulture, reviving local rites of passage that may have been lost over the years, inventing new cultures appropriate for a local steady-state community and political economy.

With these local goals accomplished and/or in thriving process, we can put forth a new, better, and less grandiose Philosophy Of Optimism (POO) (Number 2) in opposition to Leibniz, as well as to Prof. Pinker and the Pollyanna Pinkertons.

Fear Has Us Making Bad Bets on the Future

not the betting kind

  find the funky font for foolishness

where is that super swoopy f not fit for crucifying?
what's funnier than chalkduster for m.c. k⁹ to sign off with?

Zapfino has best possible f   sign off with Zapf

m.c. k⁹ looks fine accenting the doggedness Divine

fff triple forte has forceful fierceness of friend in need

    hyphenate-okay   bracing braces {   } floating free

awake with the sun

like all mornings   a wake with the sun

living the life in dry sifnos (no soaking rain the past two winters)

is small beautiful in species whose tininess is a defense
              not so easily spotted by birds or geckos or lizards?
                  haven't seen a gecko in recent visits

we watered the five olive trees last night with water from our full cistern
              twenty-seven cubic meters of water under our kitchen
        can be pumped out to grapes, figs, olive trees, to keep them healthy
through the hot and windy months of july, august, and september

if we don't come back in the fall for a few weeks
      baskim can give our permaculture a drink, some insurance, a boost,
                      another lease on life
            bukuri can keep our linens as beautiful as herself

a light on the front or side porch attracts very few moths
we hear what sounds like baby mosquitoes but experience no bites

praise minute particulars of species on dry sifnos

a backdrop, a context, a pretext, an echoic vision

a space   a pause

        some emptiness

versions of Chaos

along comes f (e# if you prefer)

with a passion to compose like an improviser

& improvise like a composer

versions of chaos fill the void

some like it   some are annoyed

angelique unique

a heavy mist and warmer outside than inside this house filled with
antecedents' detritus, sometimes known as clutter

angelique my sweetness woke up laughing and sputtering
                                   saying in Greek something about
a "question"

Q: Tee mathenoun?
A: Sto diavalo!

what are the kids learning?
devilishness!

something about who is asking and who is answering
    they are outdoors and this Q & A is funny over & over & over again

tomorrow or the next day someone will pick up the phone

& the growing well-being of all species will guide us
to a return of reverence for life

Big Showdown slowdown

prosopo vivlio
prosopo spathi
if it sounds like Greek to you
sounds like Greek to me

when electors meet
in each state
with reason and conscience
face to face

it's not just the human race
but all critters in every space
whose survival is in question
trees, grasses, grains, mushrooms too

everything could be toast
by 2020? 2022?   2122?
                    what's the future look like to you?

funny Money

funny phony identity
phony money identity
money funny identity
phony funny identity
always do my best
and leave the rest
to my deeper power

culture gets passed along
with mom's milk
and many murmurings
society permeates every message
sum up phrases
misunderstandings
all the things that don't set us free

thought a chair was a chair

only provided, he thot

PAEAN   1. Mus. A song of joyful praise or exultation.
        2. A fervent expression of joy or praise.
        3. An ancient Greek hymn of thanksgiving or invocation.

pianistic, peonistic, paeonistic, paeanistic

PAEON In quantitative verse, a foot of one long syllable and three short
syllables occurring in any order.   diBadidit 2 or 4 times to a line
                              Baadididit x times
                              didiBaadit 3 xs
                              the Beetfield paeon dididiBaa
                                                          dididiBaa
now
for us marxists it's all about the base bout da bass no superstructure now

it's about flow's gift of the c. d. wright & conversing with flow this a.m.
now
                    I'm happily centered horizontally
                                via
                        the vertical axis
                        the orthodox axis
                                wait
                        before i can go on
                    as pagan, peon, or pioneer

        i want to be the *jambazi* that holds the line & completes the sale
                        never enjamb another
            find a path to sainthood with the least collateral damage
        force words to give it up and turn loose their true meanings
                        by putting them into
                                paeans
                                  for
                                 peons
                        trickling down on the 1%

exultant
fervent
hymns for Gaia & Eternity
thanksgiving
invocation
praise
joy

Ivy League

everything rhymes
with
yale
fail
jail

new year's revolutions

{new year's revolutions}
    slow articulation   fullstoping fascism   punctuating imperialism

{braces as bows whose arrows shoot in both directions}

manifesto many festo

toward reclaiming reason and conscience
through "ignorance-based" worldview (W. Berry, W. Jackson, D. MacDonald)
from war to peace (Buddha, Diogenes, Christ, Thoreau, Gandhi, MLK, Tulsi)
from too big to fail back to small is beautiful (W. James, L. Kohr,
                                        E. F. Schumacher)
from global and regional famines back to local foods (F. M. Lappe)
from spend & consume back to save and conserve (W. Berry)
from national energy & dominance values to local energy & resilience values
                                   (R. Hopkins)
from dominator values back to partnership values (Riane Eisler)
from drama back to *dromenon* (Jane E. Harrison)
from power-over-structures back to pleasure-in-processes (Marilyn French)
from "pure" meanings to movements-feelings-meanings (Susanne Langer)
from professionals back to players (Airto)
from work back to play (J. Huizinga, David Graeber)
from commodified music back to community musicking (L. Higgins)
from alienation back to participation (Owen Barfield)
from entropy back to sacrament (Gregory Bateson)
from linear discursive back to cyclical recursive (G. Bateson)
from death wish & resistances back to life force and willingness
(S. Freud, N. O. Brown, Dorothy Dinnerstein, S. Pressfield)
from class & hierarchy back to classlessness & equality (K. Marx)
from *hubris*/tragedy back to humility/comedy (Alcoholics Anonymous)
from transcendence back to immanence (S. de Beauvoir?)
                 (from immanence to trance-in-dance)
from exclusionary thinking back to incorporative thinking (Catherine Ellis)
from utilitarian to spiritual (Jeremy Rifkin)
from spurious civilization back to genuine prime cultures (E. Sapir)
from residual to emergent (Raymond Williams)
from products back to processes (R. Williams)
from men's endless projects back to mind and Nature enough (Angie Keil)
from efficiency back to sufficiency (J. Rifkin)
from legal world back to Natural world (Haudenosaunee via John Mohawk)
from land belongs to us back to we-belong-to-land (aboriginal peoples)
from unison back to lift-up-over-sounding (Kaluli via Steve Feld)
from anarchism back to being anarchs (Semai via R. K. Dentan)
from addiction to perfection back to participatory discrepancies (C. Keil)

from dismal sciences back to joyous sciences (R. Emerson, F. Nietzsche)
from me to we (Muhammad Ali)

please fill out this list of where and how and (who inspired you) back to
where we need to go from here

space

( )
sun & moon   holding the cosmos together nurturing us, a gypsy fullstop
idea

⟨wings to make the words within   fly in all directions ⟩ a matt fox idea

meanings are lurking everywhere we just have to ferret them out, find them in
the spaces   between

so much space in the latest poetry books usually surrounds words that are
relatively meaningless
                              as if

                                        the very ratio
                    of space
                              to   words
                              in   place

makes them profound

phooey
    fu yi (rotten tofu)

convergence

didn't happen this convergence of many days before yesterday
timing estimates, trying to find the imagined "center" of public opinion
      keeps all hope on the sidelines witnessing decline
      open letters to all & sundry just a way of weighing in
      not accepting the state=us quo
               the right of King divine

minnows

taking back 9a
taking so much time
too many lawyers
in the way

penumbras and emanations
Wm Oh Douglas
did the 9th no favors
mystifications on display

fascinating fascism
captures minds
holds them hostage
let us pray

lucid & pellucid
"the Truth & Life of Myth"
a myth for each of the minnows
over 50 lost in USA up to today

the right of each minnow to live
the right of each of us to love each minnow
winnowing of the minnows
what can each of us say

revive 9a
rights to reason & conscience
rights to clean air and water
right to vote & be left alone to play

anti-Fasc

put the stirps in the stirrups for greatest possible lance leverage
into the public domains of the sustainable-resilient futures

anti-fasc as the topos for the dope in us: expel, excrete, disdain
anti-fasc as the hope, joy, light in us; adamant eve ever our game

anti-fasc, the list is long, expand, distribute, complain
anti-fasc, for the weak and strong, highlight Capital pains

Fashion Fascism

fashion fascism = hems all the same
= uniform for each functionary
= intermediate lackey sector's sizes perfected and modeled on leader's
taste
= mao jackets blue jeans torn genes same seams
= if everyone is equally evil all equally good in their equality
= big lie > pseudologics > best possible scapegoats
= being part-of-something-bigger-than-you-are made tangible
= no need to imagine your own Deeper Power
= the deepest poser easily available e.g. i.e. drumpf
=west's know-nothing narcissist perfect fit for our own-know-nothing
narcissisms
=fear of schizmogenesis
=fear of *being* without *having*
=fear of krein vs. steier in slovenian milwaukee
(they hired a swede to run the slovenian home)
=fasc could be twigs could be grass could be sticks could be plastic
swizzles
= fasc could be pastel-colored cocktails sipped while swaying to EDM in
vague-us
=could be _____

tree of life

            tree of life let me call your name
        tree of life may your photosynthesis keep us sane
            tree of life your roots our brain
            tree of life we thee reclaim
                proclaim the truth
                    of your
                    domain

draft of letter to real friend in life

i don't unfriend your wife and child
and i don't unfriend your gastrointestinal system that must be suffering
but I do unfriend your evil cortex and related ganglia

the parts of your brain that have gone vegetative
and won't let you reason the many wastes of war
the refusal to feel overpowering guilt or remorse
   for so many automated administrative massacres

Evil Hot Air

the current technofascism is fatuous
full of hot evil air
a big bad baroofa balloon that one pin prick can quickly deflate

enter The Unpresidented Brass Band
churl beating bass drum
murmuring muttering
making a point so fine it pops the balloooonbaroofa
may be your song or slogan duzit
maybe one of mine
maybe angeliki's or angelica's
fro's or dro's or somebody else's valentine

my 2 Sentences

The anti-human & anti-Nature fusion or totalizing that IS the Irrational DeathTrip we have ALL been on since 2001, should be, could be, must become, something like a Very Bad Joke that makes us smile, laugh lamely, snicker, open our eyes in mock awe, *constantly*   or, we will never defeat it.
If we are not *constantly* aware of every little advertisement, every carefully placed story, every op-ed piece's tone and details that support the totalitarian atmosphere we now breathe in and out 24/7, we will continue to swallow the dream drugs daily, we will continue to be amiably ready to take the final PatriPill when it is offered.

the clause

once we had consciousness
knew the dangers of standing armies
valued conscience and consciences
we knew reason and wrote accordingly
that government was for all the people
                            ALL the time
even the "passive" citizens were not to be screwed
for *the particular emolument or advantage*
of any single man, family OR SET OF MEN

Is there a need to approach this clause a third time?
with greater rhythm and powerful rhyme?
        & without the force of italics and capital letters all in a line?

Really Big Baby

The "irrational deathtrip" called fascism
requires man as baby
Really Big Baby as man

only an innocent baby could be so accidentally brutal
only a great man in charge can calmly say "you're fired"
and mean the meanness

The magic of Big Baby Boss
is nestled carefully
in the very in-between-ness

Drumpf as POTUS can do no wrong
always right always strong
Disagree? you're gone

obviate Fascism

the dictionary definition of obviate is prevent or avoid
postpone, undermine, devalue, piss on, deflate, don't debate: obviate

stick to the pics, the one-stroke wonders, the sultan's signatures
the let it roll dragons, the unmanned viking ships minus valkyries
the dropits, the single stroke discontinuous, the pics to piss by

obviate fascism 8 ways to sunday 9 ways beyond monday
obviate the fasc before it can form in your neck or neck of the woods
you see someone bundling twigs around an ax just say no

lift up over egalitarian as many ways as you can
see the potential in everyone
deep love in dog-eyes & holiness in every slug and snail

nonjudgement is key   we give thanks to Thee
art for celebration's sake:
"me/we" said Mr. M. Ali

●

wording the string

that ties the twigs

around the ax

www.ingramcontent.com/pod-product-compliance
Lightning Source LLC
Chambersburg PA
CBHW030309030426
42337CB00012B/644